HOW DO BEES MAKE HONEY?

Anna Claybourne

Designed by Lindy Dark

Illustrated by Sophie Allington and Annabel Spenceley

Edited by Kamini Khanduri

**Scientific consultant: James Hamill
(The Hive Honey Shop, London)**

CONTENTS

Additional illustrations by Janos Marffy

Bees and other insects

Bees are amazing insects. There are lots of different kinds, but honeybees are the most common - and they are the ones that make honey. In this book, you can find out about honeybees, and about lots of other insects.

Honeybee

Tawny mining bee

Buff-tailed bumblebee

Busy bees

Some people are frightened of honeybees, because they can sting. In fact, bees are usually busy looking for flowers, and don't sting very often.

Bees only sting if they are frightened. If you leave them alone, they probably won't hurt you.

Bees make delicious honey. On page 7, you can find out how.

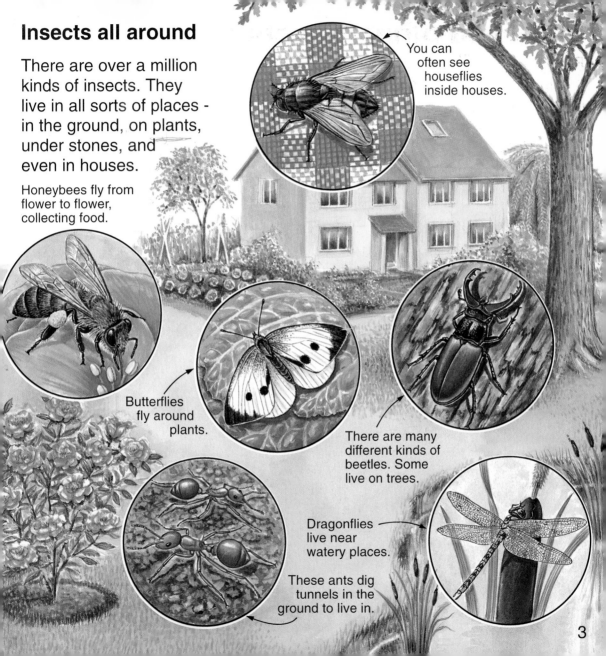

Insects all around

There are over a million kinds of insects. They live in all sorts of places - in the ground, on plants, under stones, and even in houses.

You can often see houseflies inside houses.

Honeybees fly from flower to flower, collecting food.

Butterflies fly around plants.

There are many different kinds of beetles. Some live on trees.

Dragonflies live near watery places.

These ants dig tunnels in the ground to live in.

3

A closer look

This picture shows a honeybee ten times bigger than in real life. You can see the different parts of its body.

Large wing

Small wing

A bee has a large wing and a small wing on each side. When bees fly, their wings make a buzzing sound.

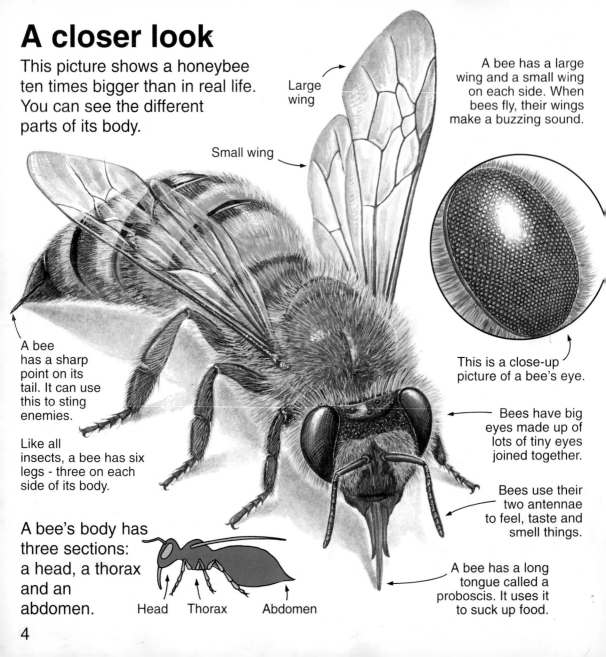

This is a close-up picture of a bee's eye.

A bee has a sharp point on its tail. It can use this to sting enemies.

Like all insects, a bee has six legs - three on each side of its body.

Bees have big eyes made up of lots of tiny eyes joined together.

Bees use their two antennae to feel, taste and smell things.

A bee's body has three sections: a head, a thorax and an abdomen.

Head   Thorax   Abdomen

A bee has a long tongue called a proboscis. It uses it to suck up food.

4

A bee or not a bee?

Lots of insects have black and yellow stripes. People sometimes mix them up with bees. Only one of these is a honeybee. Can you tell which one?

① ③ ⑤
② ④

Look on page 24 for the answer.

Bees at home

Honeybees live together in big groups called colonies. Today, most colonies live in beehives built by people.

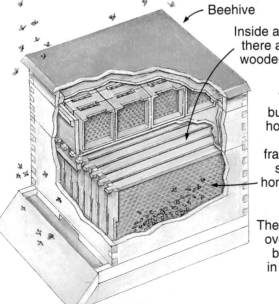

Beehive

Inside a beehive, there are lots of wooden frames.

The bees build a wax honeycomb in each frame. They store their honey there.

Wild bees' nests often hang from branches.

There can be over 50,000 bees living in one hive.

Some honeybees live in the wild. They build honeycomb nests out of wax.

5

Honey

The honey you buy in shops all comes from honeybees. They make honey as food for themselves and their babies. People take some of the honey, but they leave enough for the bees.

Honey milk shake

To make this milk shake, measure out a cupful of milk. Add a scoop of ice-cream and two teaspoons of honey.

Whisk or blend the mixture. Pour it into a glass.

Top with banana slices.

Collecting honey

People who keep bees and collect their honey are called beekeepers. They wear gloves and veils when they are working, so they do not get stung. Their clothes are white, because this makes the bees feel calm.

The beekeeper lifts each frame out of the hive, takes out the honey and puts the frame back.

Veil

Frame

You can eat honey on toast or bread. Some is used to make other things.

Honey soap

Honey cough medicine

6

How bees make honey

Honeybees make honey from a sweet liquid called nectar, which they suck out of flowers. Older bees collect the nectar and pass it on to younger bees.

Passing on nectar

This picture shows how bees make honey inside their bodies.

Honey sac

The nectar goes down a tube to the bee's stomach, or honey sac.

In the honey sac, the nectar gets thicker and turns into honey.

The honey comes out through the bee's mouth. It is kept safe in the hive.

Different kinds

Different kinds of honey come from different flowers.

Apple blossom honey is thick and yellow.

Borage flower honey is pale and runny.

Next time you go to the shops, you could look for different kinds of honey. How many can you find?

Bees and flowers

On warm days, female honeybees visit flowers to collect nectar and a kind of yellow powder called pollen. They use pollen as food for their babies.

The bee lands on the flower and sticks her proboscis, or tongue, into the middle to reach the nectar.

Honeybee

Petals

Tiny drops of nectar are hidden in little hollows at the bottom of the flower's petals.

Pollen is found on little stalks, called stamens, in the middle of the flower.

Some pollen s to the bee's legs and body. She rolls it into balls which she carries on her back legs.

Busy helpers

Flowers need to swap pollen with each other to produce seeds. Bees and other insects carry pollen from one flower to the next. This is called pollination.

... visiting a ... gets ... in specks of pollen.

When the bumblebee flies to another dog rose, she carries some pollen with her.

The pollen helps the second dog rose make seeds which can grow into new dog roses.

...ing a beeline

... bright markings ... These attract ... to pollinate the flower. Some flowers ... dark lines called honeyguides.

Mountain pansy →

Honeyguides →

Scientists think that honeyguides may help insects find their way into flowers.

Flower feeders

It's not just bees that like flowers. Many other insects, such as butterflies, visit flowers to feed on nectar.

Monarch butterfly feeding on nectar

Inside a beehive

This picture shows part of a honeycomb inside a beehive. It is made up of lots of little compartments called cells. There are three types of honeybees in a hive.

Worker bees are all females. They do lots of jobs, such as collecting food, making honey and looking after baby bees.

Drones are big male bees. Their job is to mate with a queen from another hive.

Powerful perfume

The queen gives off a smell called a pheromone. This makes the other bees calm and happy, because they know their queen is safe.

Smell coming from queen

The queen bee lays eggs to make new bees for the hive.

The worker bees buzz around the queen.

Making cells

Worker bees build cells from wax, which they make in their stomachs. The wax comes out in flakes under their bodies.

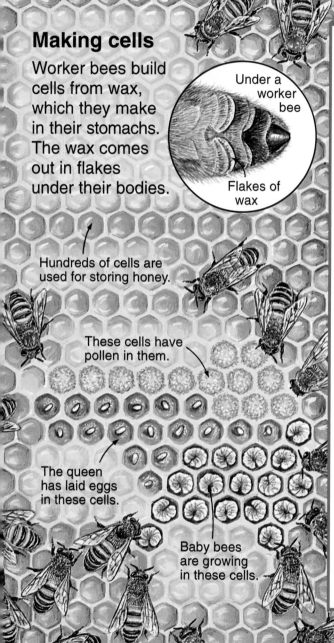

Hundreds of cells are used for storing honey.

These cells have pollen in them.

The queen has laid eggs in these cells.

Baby bees are growing in these cells.

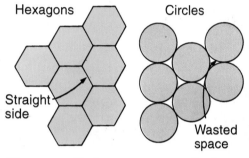

Under a worker bee

Flakes of wax

Useful shapes

The cells in a hive are almost round, but not quite. Honeybees give the cells six straight sides. Can you guess why this shape is better than a round shape?

Hexagons

Circles

Straight side

Wasted space

These cell shapes are called hexagons. Hexagons fit together well. This means the bees can build lots of cells next to each other, with no wasted space.

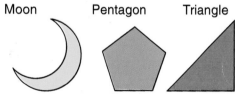

Moon

Pentagon

Triangle

Can you see which of these shapes would fit together like hexagons? Find out on page 24.

13

Living in groups

Honeybees are not the only insects that live in groups - many other kinds do too. Insects that live together are called social insects.

Queens and kings

Social insects usually have a queen. She lays eggs for the colony and is often bigger than the other insects.

A wasp queen is nearly twice as big as the other wasps.

A termite queen is much bigger than the other termites. Her abdomen is so full of eggs, she cannot move.

Worker termites look after their queen and bring her food.

Termites have a king too, but he is much smaller than the queen.

Sharing food

Most social insects share food. These leafcutter ants are carrying bits of leaf back to their nest to make a store.

Leafcutter ants cut pieces out of leaves with their jaws.

An ant can carry a piece of leaf bigger than its own body.

Termite towers

Social insects often build themselves a home to share. Termites build tall towers out of soil, saliva (spit) and droppings. The termites live in the bottom part of the tower.

This picture shows the tunnels and tiny rooms inside the tower.

A termite tower can be up to 9m (30ft) high - much taller than a giraffe.

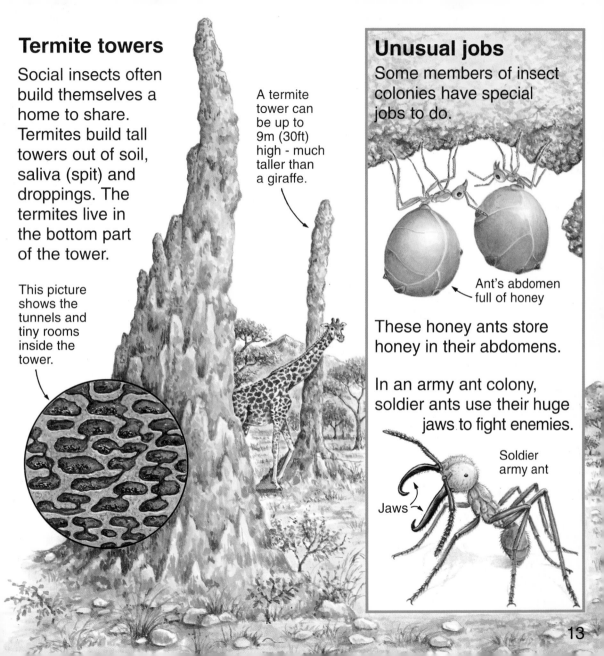

Unusual jobs

Some members of insect colonies have special jobs to do.

Ant's abdomen full of honey

These honey ants store honey in their abdomens.

In an army ant colony, soldier ants use their huge jaws to fight enemies.

Soldier army ant

Jaws

13

Baby insects

All baby insects hatch out of eggs. Many of them look completely different from the adults.

Becoming a butterfly

Baby butterflies are called caterpillars. They have to change a lot before they can become adults.

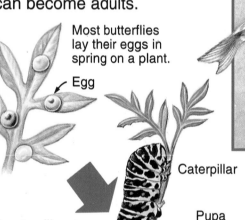

Most butterflies lay their eggs in spring on a plant.

Egg

Caterpillar

A caterpillar hatches out of each egg. It feeds on the plant during the summer.

In autumn, the caterpillar grows a hard shell called a pupa. Inside, it changes very slowly.

Pupa

Dragonflies lay their eggs in water. When the babies hatch out, they live underwater for up to five years. Baby dragonflies, or nymphs, are small but very fierce.

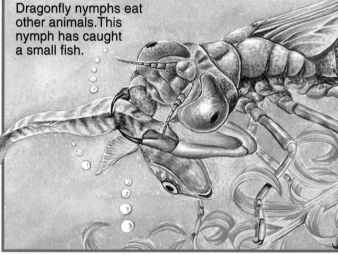

Dragonfly nymphs eat other animals. This nymph has caught a small fish.

When it breaks out of the pupa a few months later, the caterpillar has changed into a butterfly.

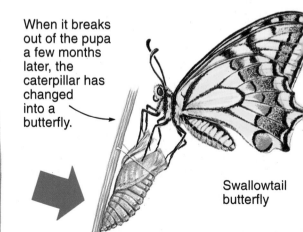

Swallowtail butterfly

14

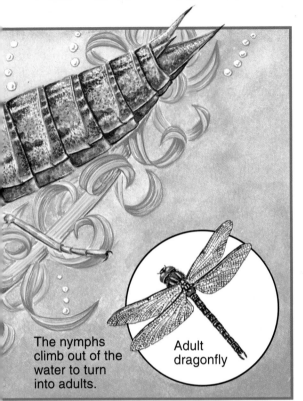

The nymphs climb out of the water to turn into adults.

Adult dragonfly

Which is which?

Can you tell which caterpillar turns into which butterfly? Follow the lines to find out.

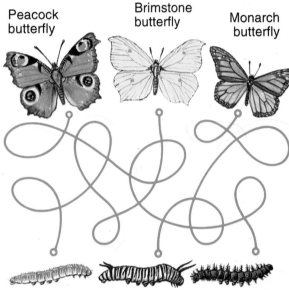

Peacock butterfly

Brimstone butterfly

Monarch butterfly

Feeding time

Some kinds of baby insects need to be fed by adults, but many can look after themselves.

This worker honeybee is bringing food to a baby in its cell. Baby bees, called larvae (say 'lar-vee'), can't fly or even crawl.

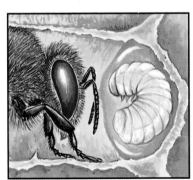

The caterpillars of large white butterflies find their own food. They can eat whole fields of crops.

Cabbage

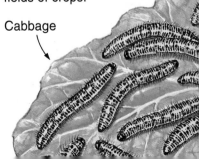

Hunters

Some insects hunt other animals to eat. Many hunting insects use clever tricks or secret traps to catch their food. The animals they catch are called prey.

Surprise attack

Mantises hunt by sneaking up on their prey and taking it by surprise.

Mantises have big, strong front legs for grabbing prey.

This mantis is leaping out of its leafy hiding place to catch a honeybee.

The mantis's green body makes it hard to see among the leaves.

The mantis tears its prey apart and eats it up slowly.

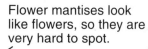

Flower mantises look like flowers, so they are very hard to spot.

Digging a trap

Antlions catch their prey by trapping it. They dig a hole and hide at the bottom.

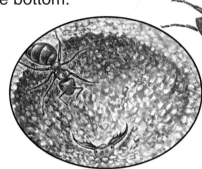

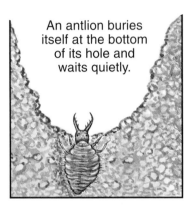

An antlion buries itself at the bottom of its hole and waits quietly.

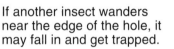

If another insect wanders near the edge of the hole, it may fall in and get trapped.

Then the antlion suddenly jumps out of the sand, grabs the insect and eats it up.

Liquid lunch

An assassin bug squirts a special juice into its prey, using its hard, pointed tongue. The juice turns the prey's insides into liquid, which the assassin bug sucks out.

Blood suckers

Mosquitoes feed on the blood of people and other animals. They stick their long, sharp tongues into their prey's skin and suck out some blood.

A mosquito sucking blood from a person's arm.

17

Staying safe

Because they are so small, insects are always in danger of being eaten or attacked by other animals. They have different ways of staying safe.

Stinging attack

Honeybees often scare away enemies by stinging them. Bees die after stinging, so they don't do it unless they are very scared.

Warning signals

Sometimes, bright markings can tell enemies that an insect tastes bad or is poisonous.

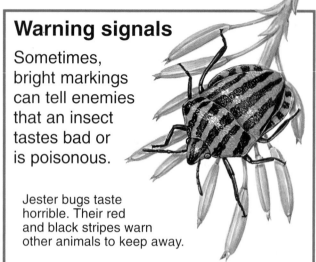

Jester bugs taste horrible. Their red and black stripes warn other animals to keep away.

Bees usually sting to protect the other bees and larvae in their colony.

This bear has tried to steal honey from a beehive. Some of the bees are chasing after the bear and stinging it.

This bee is stinging a person. It injects its poison into the skin.

18

Bombardiers

If a bombardier beetle is attacked, it sprays its enemy with hot gas from the end of its abdomen. The gas hurts the enemy's eyes and skin. This bombardier beetle is spraying gas at a frog.

The beetle can spray very suddenly and in any direction.

Hot gas

When it feels the painful hot gas, the frog will probably leave the beetle alone.

Find the insects

Some insects match their surroundings, so they can hide easily. This is called camouflage.

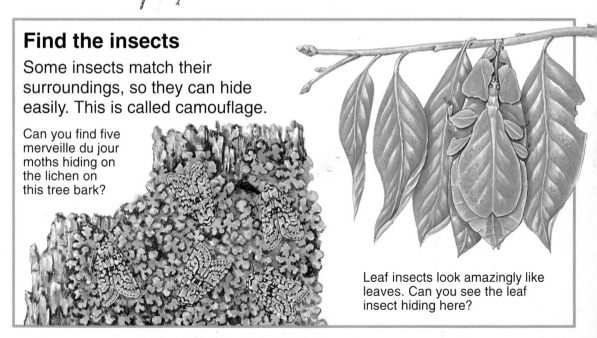

Can you find five merveille du jour moths hiding on the lichen on this tree bark?

Leaf insects look amazingly like leaves. Can you see the leaf insect hiding here?

Sending messages

Insects can't talk to each other in words, like people do, but they can send messages and signals in lots of different ways.

Floral dances

When a honeybee has found a patch of flowers, she goes back to the hive and does a dance to tell the other bees about it.

This dance is called the round dance. It means the food is nearby.

The dancing bee goes around in a circle, first one way, then the other.

This dance is called the waggle dance. It means the food is quite far away.

The faster the bee waggles her tail, the nearer the food is.

← Path of bee

Metal messenger

Robot bee

This robot bee doesn't look much like a real bee, but it can dance so that real bees understand it. Scientists use it to find out how bees send messages.

20

Keeping in touch

Insects use their antennae to pick up messages and signals.

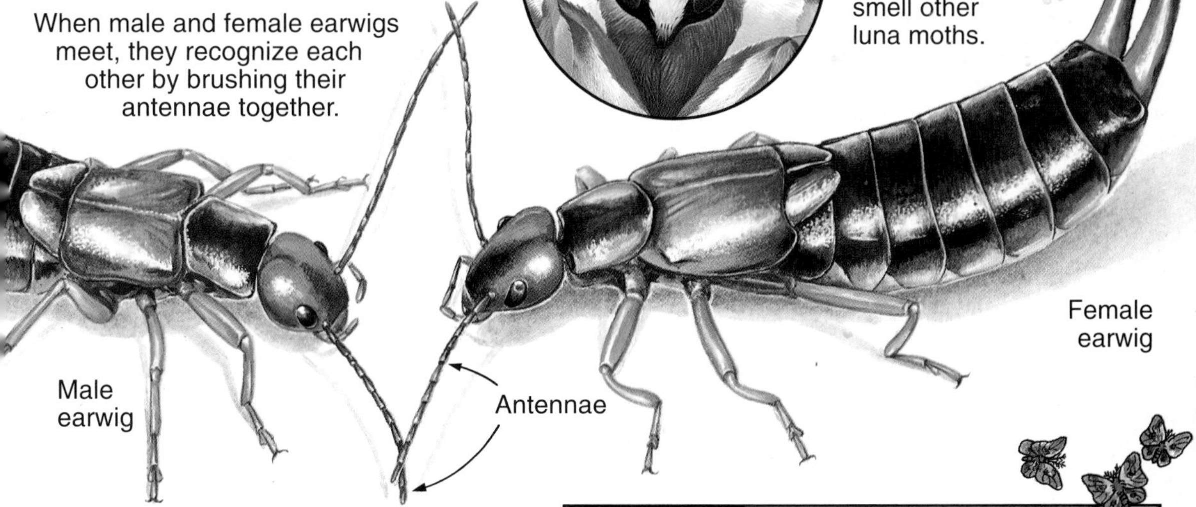

When male and female earwigs meet, they recognize each other by brushing their antennae together.

This close-up picture shows a luna moth's feathery antennae. It uses them to smell other luna moths.

Female earwig

Male earwig

Antennae

Long-distance love

Some moths give out a special smell when they want a mate. A scientist named Fabré discovered this over a hundred years ago.

One day, Fabré caught a female emperor moth and put her in a cage in his study.

That evening, Fabré was amazed to find the room full of large male emperor moths.

The male moths had smelled the female and come to find her.

21

Insects and people

Many people think that insects are a nuisance. Some insects do cause problems by biting people or eating crops, but others can be very useful.

Honey in history

People have been eating honey for a very long time. The wall painting in this picture is over 7,000 years old. It shows a woman collecting honey from a honeybees' nest.

Nest

The honey collector has climbed a tree to reach the bees' nest.

Basket for honey

Bees

Cloth from a moth

Silk comes from the caterpillars of the silk moth. The caterpillars, called silkworms, spin thread around themselves.

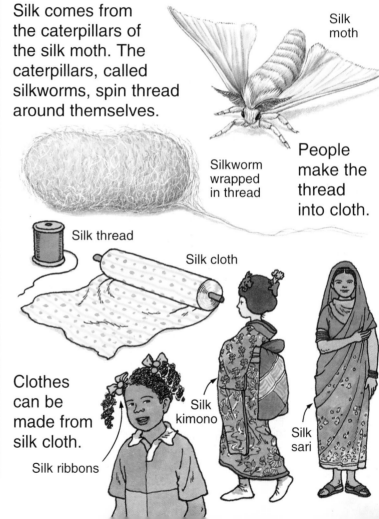

Silk moth

Silkworm wrapped in thread

People make the thread into cloth.

Silk thread

Silk cloth

Clothes can be made from silk cloth.

Silk ribbons

Silk kimono

Silk sari

On the farm

Some insects eat the crops that farmers grow. In Africa, locusts are a big problem.

In one day, a large swarm of locusts can eat enough food for millions of people.

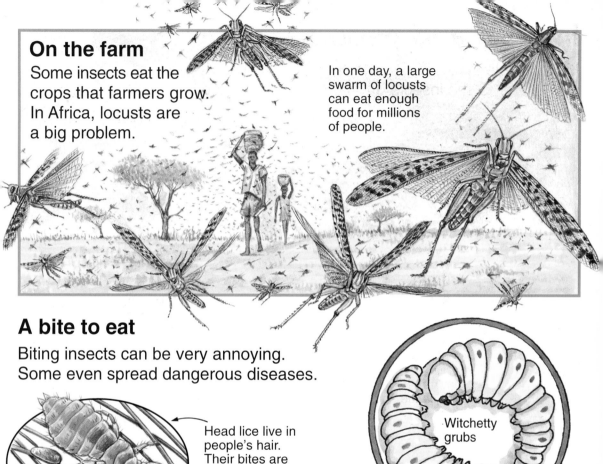

A bite to eat

Biting insects can be very annoying. Some even spread dangerous diseases.

Head lice live in people's hair. Their bites are very itchy, and they lay tiny eggs called nits.

Nit

When tsetse flies bite people or animals, they can give them a very bad disease called sleeping sickness.

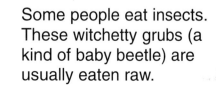

Witchetty grubs

Some people eat insects. These witchetty grubs (a kind of baby beetle) are usually eaten raw.

23

Index

Quiz answers

Page 5 - Number 4 is the honeybee. Number 1 is a fly, number 2 is a beetle, number 3 is a wasp and number 5 is a moth.

Page 11 - Only triangles would fit together with no wasted space.

First published in 1994 by Usborne Publishing Ltd, 83-85 Saffron Hill, London EC1N 8RT, England. Copyright © 1994 Usborne Publishing Ltd.